Hands

By Cynthia Klingel and Robert B. Noyed

Reading consultant: Cecilia Minden-Cupp, Ph.D.,
Adjunct Professor, College of Continuing and Professional Studies, University of Virginia

Gareth Stevens
Publishing

Please visit our Web site www.garethstevens.com. For a free color catalog of all our high-quality books, call toll free 1-800-542-2595 or fax 1-877-542-2596.

Library of Congress Cataloging-in-Publication Data

Klingel, Cynthia.
    Hands / by Cynthia Klingel and Robert B. Noyed.
      p. cm. – (Let's read about our bodies)
    Includes bibliographical references and index.
    Summary: An introduction to hands, what they are used for, and how to take care of them.
    ISBN: 978-1-4339-3365-3 (lib. bdg.)
    ISBN: 978-1-4339-3366-0 (pbk.)
    ISBN: 978-1-4339-3367-7 (6-pack)
    1. Hand–Juvenile literature. [1. Hand.] I. Noyed, Robert B. II. Title.
  QM548.K554 2002
  611'.97–dc21
                                       2001055092

New edition published 2010 by
Gareth Stevens Publishing
111 East 14th Street, Suite 349
New York, NY 10003

New text and images this edition copyright © 2010 Gareth Stevens Publishing

Original edition published 2003 by Weekly Reader® Books
An imprint of Gareth Stevens Publishing
Original edition text and images copyright © 2003 Gareth Stevens Publishing

Art direction: Haley Harasymiw, Tammy Gruenewald
Page layout: Daniel Hosek, Katherine A. Goedheer
Editorial direction: Kerri O'Donnell, Diane Laska Swanke

Photo credits: Cover iStockphoto.com; pp. 5, 9, 11, 13, 15, 17, 19 Gregg Andersen; pp. 7, 9, 21 shutterstock.com.

Printed in the United States of America

CPSIA compliance information: Batch #WW10GS: For further information contact Gareth Stevens, New York, New York at 1-800-542-2595.

Table of Contents

My Hands 4

Hands at Work 12

Caring for Hands 16

Let's Count! 20

Glossary 22

For More Information 23

Index 24

Boldface words appear in the glossary.

My Hands

These are my hands.

I have two hands.

I have ten fingers.
I have five fingers
on each hand.

I have ten **fingernails**. I keep them short and clean.

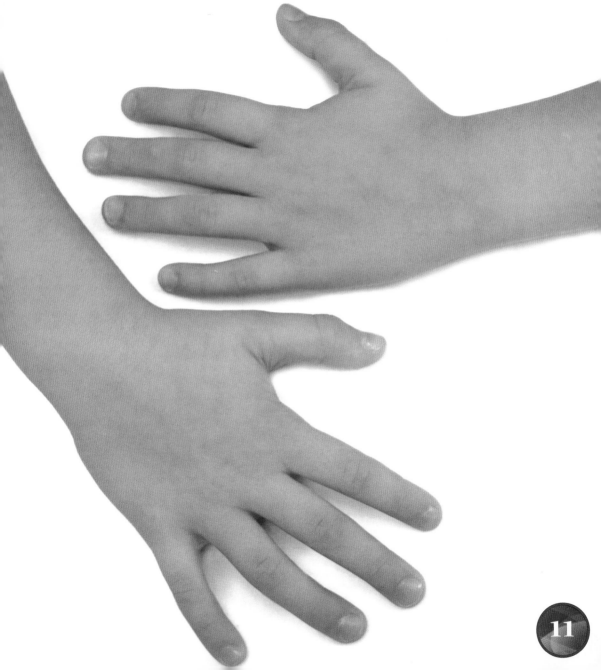

Hands at Work

I use my hands
to pick up toys.

I use my hands
to **clap**.

Caring for Hands

I wear **mittens** when it is cold. Mittens keep my hands warm.

I keep my hands clean. I wash them with soap and water.

Let's Count!

I can even count
with my hands!
Can you?

Glossary

clap: to strike your hands together for enjoyment

fingernails: a thin, hard layer of material that grows at the end of each finger

mittens: coverings worn on the hands to keep them warm

For More Information

Books

Agassi, Martine. *Hands Are Not for Hitting.* Minneapolis, MN: Free Spirit Publishing, 2009.

Ehlert, Lois. *Hands: Growing Up to Be an Artist.* New York: Harcourt Children's Books, 2004.

Ross, Tony. *Wash Your Hands!* La Jolla, CA: Kane/Miller Book Publishers, 2006.

Royston, Angela. *Why Do I Wash My Hands?* London: QED Publishing, 2010.

Web Sites

Why Do I Need to Wash My Hands?

kidshealth.org/kid/talk/qa/wash_hands.html

For information about why you should wash your hands

Index

caring for 10, 16, 18
clapping 14
cleaning 10, 18
counting 20
fingernails 10

fingers 8
keeping warm 16
mittens 16
washing 18

About the Authors

Cynthia Klingel has worked as a high school English teacher and an elementary school teacher. She is currently the curriculum director for a Minnesota school district. Cynthia Klingel lives with her family in Mankato, Minnesota.

Robert B. Noyed started his career as a newspaper reporter. Since then, he has worked in school communications and public relations at the state and national level. Robert B. Noyed lives with his family in Brooklyn Center, Minnesota.